RAISING the FLAG on IWO JIMA

written by **Nel Yomtov**

illustrated by **Eduardo Garcia**

CAPSTONE PRESS
a capstone imprint

Published by Capstone Press, an imprint of Capstone
1710 Roe Crest Drive, North Mankato, Minnesota 56003
capstonepub.com

Library of Congress Cataloging-in-Publication Data
Names: Yomtov, Nel, author. | Garcia, Eduardo, 1970 August 31- illustrator.
Title: Raising the flag on Iwo Jima / by Nel Yomtov ; illustrated by Eduardo Garcia.
Description: North Mankato, Minesota : Capstone Press, [2024] | Series: Great moments in history | Includes bibliographical references. | Audience: Ages 8 to 11 | Audience: Grades 4–6 | Summary: "On February 23, 1945, an American flag was raised atop Mount Suribachi on the Japanese island of Iwo Jima. The moment-captured in one of the most famous photographs of all time-didn't just boost the morale of the U.S. soldiers fighting on the island. It also lifted the spirits of the American people back home who had grown weary of World War II. How did this remarkable moment come to pass and what is its enduring legacy? Find out in an easy-to-read graphic novel that reveals why the flag raising on Iwo Jima is among the greatest moments in history"—Provided by publisher.
Identifiers: LCCN 2022047825 (print) | LCCN 2022047826 (ebook) | ISBN 9781669017134 (hardcover) | ISBN 9781669017080 (paperback) | ISBN 9781669017097 (pdf) | ISBN 9781669017110 (kindle edition) | ISBN 9781669017127 (epub)
Subjects: LCSH: Iwo Jima, Battle of, Japan, 1945—Juvenile literature. | Iwo Jima, Battle of, Japan, 1945—Comic books, strips, etc. | Graphic novels.
Classification: LCC D767.99.I9 Y66 2024 (print) | LCC D767.99.I9 (ebook) | DDC 940.54/2428—dc23/eng/20221004
LC record available at https://lccn.loc.gov/2022047825
LC ebook record available at https://lccn.loc.gov/2022047826

Editorial Credits
Editor: Christopher Harbo; Designer: Tracy Davies; Production Specialist: Katy LaVigne

Design Element by Shutterstock/kzww

All internet sites appearing in back matter were available and accurate when this book was sent to press.

Direct quotations appear in bold italicized text on the following pages:
Page 9, from "Closing In: Marines in the Seizure of Iwo Jima" by Colonel Joseph H. Alexander (marines.mil, 2009).
Page 17, from *Investigating Iwo: The Flag Raisings in Myth, Memory, & Esprit de Corps* by Breanne Robertson, ed. (Marine Corps History Division, 2019).
Page 18, from *Flags of Our Fathers: Heroes of Iwo Jima* by James Bradley and Ron Powers (Bantam, 2000).
Page 22, from "Bay Area Photographer's Iwo Jima Photo Still Resonates After 75 Years" by Matthew Pera (*The Mercury News*, February 24, 2020).

Printed and bound in China 5379

Table of Contents

Introduction   The Road to Japan

On December 7, 1941, Japanese warplanes launched a surprise attack on the U.S. naval base at Pearl Harbor, Hawaii.

Five U.S. battleships and three destroyers were sunk. Nearly 150 aircraft were destroyed. More than 2,300 military personnel were killed and more than 1,500 wounded.

For the first two years of World War II (1939–1945), the United States had avoided the fighting happening in Europe and the Pacific. But on December 8, the United States declared war on Japan.

The Japanese military quickly took advantage of their success at Pearl Harbor. They expanded their control throughout the Pacific.

And despite bitter and brutal fighting against the United States and its allies, Japan's war industries at home remained in full production.

The United States had to find a way to stop Japan's ability to wage war. The answer was the B-29 Superfortress bomber.

That bird will bring Japan to its knees.

And avoid us having to invade the island, which would cost us tens of thousands of our boys' lives.

The giant bomber had a range of more than 5,000 miles (8,000 kilometers).

By late 1944, U.S. forces had seized the Pacific islands of Guam, Saipan, and Tinian.

Flying from runways on these islands, B-29s pounded the Japanese mainland.

The tiny island of Iwo Jima was even closer to Japan. It had two Japanese airfields and a third under construction.

The United States needed to win control of the island and seize the airfields.

General Tadamichi Kuribayashi commanded the Japanese forces on Iwo Jima. Preparing for a U.S. attack, he created a nearly impenetrable system of defense on the island.

Unknown to U.S. forces, as many as 23,000 Japanese troops were hiding in miles of underground tunnels, bunkers, and caves. A vast network of pillboxes and bunkers with machine guns, riflemen, antitank guns, and mortars crisscrossed the island.

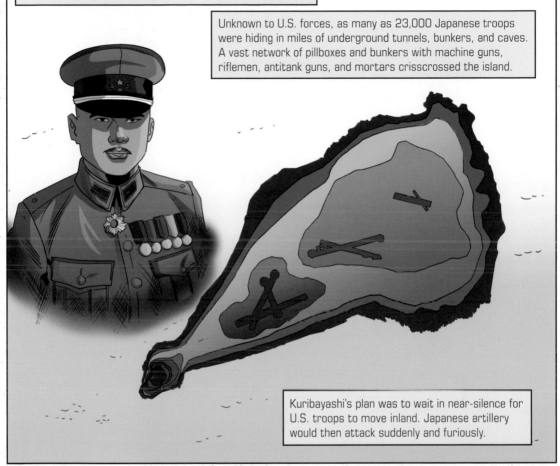

Kuribayashi's plan was to wait in near-silence for U.S. troops to move inland. Japanese artillery would then attack suddenly and furiously.

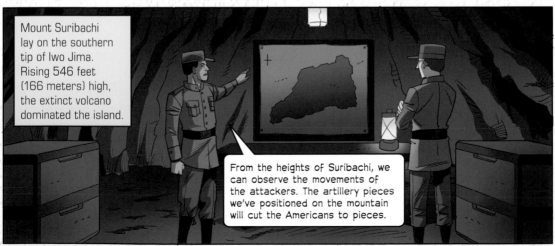

Mount Suribachi lay on the southern tip of Iwo Jima. Rising 546 feet (166 meters) high, the extinct volcano dominated the island.

From the heights of Suribachi, we can observe the movements of the attackers. The artillery pieces we've positioned on the mountain will cut the Americans to pieces.

U.S. commanders met to discuss the battle plan.

Our success depends on seizing control of Suribachi quickly. Then we can use the mountain to our advantage.

Marines will come in from the sea and land on the island's southwestern beach, here. They are to storm Suribachi and crush the enemy defenders. This will cut off the mountain from the rest of the island.

Other marine divisions will fight to secure Airfield One. Then they'll begin the push into the heart of the island.

Beginning on December 8, 1944, B-29 Superfortresses and B-24 Liberators battered Iwo Jima mercilessly.

The heavy bombing encouraged some U.S. commanders.

Once our troops land, Iwo Jima will fall in four days, tops.

Possibly sooner.

Little did they know that the fighting would rage for a month after the landings, or that one of the most famous photographs in U.S. history would soon be taken.

Chapter 1 Assault!

On February 15, 1945, the U.S. invasion fleet left Saipan. Nearly 500 battleships, cruisers, and destroyers churned their way to Iwo Jima.

The fleet included hundreds of landing craft called amtracs and landing ship, tanks (LSTs). Amtracs carried troops and a howitzer for firing shells. LSTs carried tanks, vehicles, cargo, and troops.

The force totaled about 60,000 marines. It was the largest force of U.S. Marines ever sent into a single battle.

Beginning on February 16, the offshore fleet blasted the island for three days to prepare for the landing.

Meanwhile, on Iwo Jima, General Kuribayashi was in his headquarters 75 feet (23 m) below ground.

U.S. planes flying from aircraft carriers stationed in the Pacific flew hundreds of bombing missions over the island. And yet, there was no sign of the Japanese on Iwo Jima.

On February 19, the first amtracs hit the landing beach at about 9:00 a.m. Hundreds more were behind them. The crafts met almost no resistance from the Japanese.

Instead, the first wave of attackers was stopped dead in its tracks by the island itself. Vehicles got stuck in the soft black volcanic ash and could not move.

We're barely moving in this stuff!

Loaded with heavy equipment, troops sank ankle-deep into the sand with every step.

It's like trying to run in loose coffee grounds!

The delays caused the landing beaches to back up with boats and vehicles. Waves filled boats with water and sand, turning them over.

One of the ships waiting to land was USS *LST-181*. It carried soldiers of the 28th Marine Regiment of the 5th Division. The 28th was given the job of cutting off Suribachi from the rest of the island and capturing it.

You figure we're gonna make it out alive?

No idea, but it can't hurt to say a prayer, eh?

Shortly after 9:00 a.m., Japanese guns suddenly opened fire on the Americans.

BADOOM!

KROOM!

Cannons blasted out from hidden caves and command posts.

Shells, mortars, and machine gun rounds rained down on the Americans. With nowhere to go and no cover, casualties were very high.

We walked into a trap! They've been waiting for us all along!

Keep your head down--or you're gonna lose it!

By evening about 30,000 marine troops had landed, including the men of the 28th.

We lost a lot of boys today. I have a feeling it's only going to get worse.

For the next three days, the men of the 28th battled the Japanese defenders at the base of Suribachi. Both sides suffered tremendous casualties. But by February 22, the marines had the Japanese surrounded.

Colonel Harry Liversedge was the commanding officer of the 28th Marines. On the afternoon of February 22, he met with Lieutenant Colonel Chandler Johnson, one of his battalion commanders.

I've just received orders to seize and occupy the mountain peak, Colonel Chandler.

Tomorrow, we climb!

Chapter 2 A Flag Is Raised

On the morning of February 23 . . .

For days, the Japanese from Suribachi tore up our boys fighting on the rest of the island. This morning's scouting party found no sign of the enemy on the mountain. They must have abandoned their positions.

That's good news. But we need to let the men across the island know when a force reaches and secures the summit. A sign of some sort will keep up their morale.

How about flares or lighting smoke pots?

Raising an American flag would be a powerful and meaningful symbol to our boys.

Excellent idea, Colonel Johnson. I have only one requirement.

I want a highly capable officer to lead the patrol to the summit. First Lieutenant Schrier will be the man.

Lieutenant Harold Schrier was among the 28th Marines' most experienced officers. Earlier in the war, he had fought on Guadalcanal and other Pacific battlefields.

The Japanese army seemed to have disappeared from the mountain. But some U.S. commanders believed they were hiding and waiting for a larger force to arrive. Before the U.S. patrol set out, Suribachi was bombarded yet again.

Meanwhile . . .

If you get to the top, put it up, Lieutenant Schrier.

Yessir, Colonel Johnson.

The flag came from the USS *Missoula*, one of the transport ships. It measured 54 by 28 inches (137 by 71 centimeters).

As Schrier and his 40-man patrol prepared to climb, he was interrupted by a familiar voice.

You mind if I tag along, Lieutenant?

No problem, Lou. Be our guest.

Louis Lowery was a Marine staff sergeant and photographer for *Leatherneck* magazine. He wanted to take photos of the climb up Suribachi.

I've got a feeling we're not going to make it.

It's much too quiet.

You're in charge of the flag, Private Ward.

By 10:00 a.m., the patrol reached the crater of the volcano. Not a single shot was fired.

The men's attention turned to raising the flag.

We found a piece of pipe to use as a flagpole, Lieutenant!

Good work, men! Pass it up here!

The flag was unfolded and tied to the pole. At 10:20 a.m., marines thrust the pole upright into the soft volcanic ash. This American flag was the first foreign flag to fly over Japanese territory during World War II.

Lou Lowery took a series of photos of the flag raisers' progress.

U.S. soldiers on the beach rejoiced when they saw the flag flying high.

Look! We got Suribachi!

Woo-hoo! Way to go, boys!

The shores and ships below Suribachi erupted in celebration. Vessels of all types and sizes blared horns to honor the small group of men who raised the flag.

Suddenly, the mountaintop came alive with Japanese defenders. The Americans blasted away at the cave entrances from which the Japanese appeared.

Fire! Take cover and fire!

BADOOM!

Within minutes, the threat was wiped out. But the attack was a reminder that the inspirational flag raising was just a brief pause in the dangerous task of defeating a deadly foe. The flag raisers knew it was time to get back to work.

Chapter 3 The Second Flag

The flag raising captured the attention of important U.S. personnel. U.S. Secretary of Defense James Forrestal had traveled to Iwo Jima to support the troops. Minutes after the flag raising, he met with General Holland "Howlin' Mad" Smith, who commanded one of the marine units on the island.

The raising of that flag means a lot to the Marine Corps. I'd like that flag for a souvenir, Holland.

Please send a message to Colonel Johnson and tell him I want the flag.

Yessir, Mr. Secretary.

Of all the crazy things! Forrestal wants the flag for himself! That flag belongs to our unit--the guys who risked their lives to put it up!

Go to the beach and rustle up another flag for Forrestal, Lieutenant Tuttle.

Wait, I've got an idea! Find a bigger flag. We'll swap it out for the one that's already up.

Back on Suribachi, photographer Joe Rosenthal had just arrived on Iwo Jima. Rosenthal worked for the Associated Press news service. He heard about the flag raising and wanted to take photos of the marines on the mountain.

It's too late to photograph the flag raising, Joe, but I'm happy to take you to the summit.

Thanks, Sergeant Genaust. I'd still like to go up.

Besides, I want to take some color film with my movie camera from the top of Suribachi.

Meanwhile, Tuttle was on a mission.

What do you need a flag for, soldier?

Communication officer Alan Wood secured a flag for Tuttle. Measuring 96 by 56 inches (244 x 142 cm), it was much larger than the one planted on the mountain.

Thanks, pal. You won't regret it.

The flag had been rescued from a ship the Japanese had sunk at Pearl Harbor.

Good work, Tuttle. I'll send the flag up with these men of the 28th. They're going to run a telephone wire up to the summit so I can communicate with Colonel Schrier.

They'll also be bringing the colonel a fresh supply of batteries for his backpack–mounted walkie–talkie.

Corporal Harlon Block

Private First Class René Gagnon

Private First Class Ira Hayes

Private First Class Franklin Sousley

Sergeant Mike Strank

Put this in your field pack, Gagnon.

Strank, when you get to the top, tell Schrier to put this flag up, and I want him to save the small flag for me.

Okay, Colonel, will do.

Around noon, the group reached the top of Suribachi with their delivery of wire, batteries, and the flag.

Colonel Johnson wants this big flag run up high, Lieutenant Schrier, so that everyone on this whole crummy island can see it!

Hayes, you and Sousley go look for another piece of pipe. Block and I will start clearing a space for the pole.

Got it, Sarge. Shouldn't be hard to find among all this junk.

Rosenthal! Sergeant Genaust! I photographed the flag raising. But you should go on up there. There are good shots to be had. You can see the whole beach with the ships and equipment.

Thanks, Lou. No sense in turning back now, anyway.

Hey! Looks like there's going to be a second flag raising. Maybe I can get a good shot of this!

I want your team to do the job, Strank. Put up this flag as you're lowering the first one.

Got it, Colonel.

As Strank's team prepared to raise the flag, Rosenthal and Genaust set up their vantage point to get a good photograph.

There it goes, Bill!

Rosenthal quickly snapped the shutter of his camera.

He almost missed the shot because he and Genaust were trying extra hard not to get in each other's way.

CLICK!

Rosenthal had no idea if he had gotten a good photo or not. Nor did Sergeant Genaust, who took color footage with his movie camera. Rosenthal would have to wait until his film was developed many hours later to see the results of his work.

In the rush of the moment, no one recorded the names of the other flag raisers. This error would cause considerable confusion in the months and years ahead.

The fighting and bloodshed raged throughout Iwo Jima. Within days, two of the flag raisers—Strank and Sousley—were killed in action on the island.

Chapter 4 A Nation Responds

Rosenthal needed to provide descriptions of the 18 photos he had taken that day. He wrote the captions for his undeveloped film.

He sent his film out to a ship offshore. It was then flown to Guam, 800 miles (1,287 km) away, to be developed.

The film was developed by Associated Press editors, along with the photos of many other correspondents covering the war in the Pacific. One particular photo caught the eye of editor John Bodkin. It was Rosenthal's.

Here's one for all time!

Rosenthal's photo was sent to the United States by electronic wirephoto. It arrived at the Associated Press offices in minutes.

Louis Lowery, the photographer of the first flag raising, sent out his film with the press boat that night.

The film was flown back to the United States. By that time, Rosenthal's photo was already making big headlines back home.

The first news report of a flag raising appeared in an Associated Press story in the *Boston Daily Globe*. The story ran on the same day, February 23, 1945.

Two days later, the *New York Times* published Rosenthal's photo for the first time under the headline OLD GLORY GOES UP OVER IWO. In part, the article read, "The planting of the American flag two days ago marked a definite change in American fortunes on Iwo Jima."

These early reports made no mention of the first flag raising.

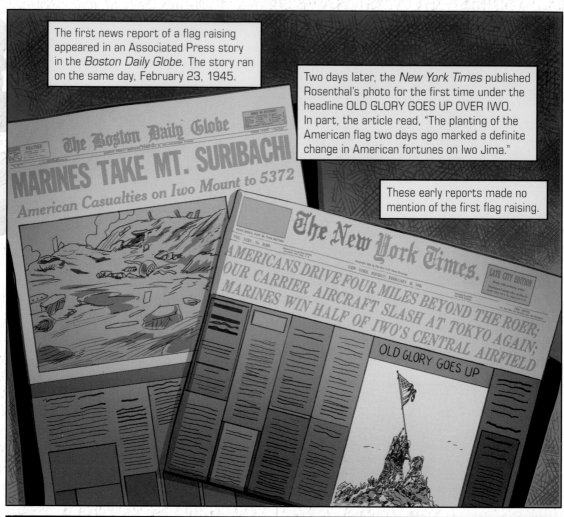

Rosenthal's photo was printed in thousands of papers and magazines across the nation. Most Americans assumed there was only one flag raising.

Rosenthal—thousands of miles away on Iwo Jima—became an instant celebrity.

Americans—including President Franklin Delano Roosevelt—wanted to know who raised the second flag.

Identify the six flagmen and recall them to the United States, General. I want them to participate in the 7th War Loan drive.

Yessir, Mr. President!

War bond drives were campaigns to encourage Americans to buy U.S. Treasury bonds to help finance World War II. Radio, newspapers, and magazines urged citizens to support the war effort.

$18,300,000

The raisers of the second flag were identified as Henry Hansen, René Gagnon, John Bradley, Mike Strank, Ira Hayes, and Franklin Sousley.

Only Bradley, Gagnon, and Hayes could participate in the drive. Hansen had been injured in combat, and Strank and Sousley were killed in action.

7 WAR LOAN ALL TOGETHER

The tour kicked off on May 9, 1945. The three men appeared at massive events across the country. They gave speeches and participated in flag-raising reenactments.

The marines became national celebrities. The war bond drive raised more than $14 billion for the U.S. war effort (about $227 billion in today's dollars).

Rosenthal's image quickly became part of American culture. It was reproduced on belt buckles, T-shirts, posters, coffee mugs, dishes, and more. It inspired movies and novels. In July 1945, a postage stamp was released featuring a painting of the photo.

The United States finally captured Iwo Jima on March 26, 1945—36 days after the fighting began. In all, nearly 7,000 U.S. soldiers died and more than 19,000 were wounded.

Then in August, U.S. B-29s dropped two atomic bombs on the Japanese cities of Hiroshima and Nagasaki. On September 2, Japan formally surrendered to the Allies. World War II was over.

Chapter 5

An Enduring Legacy

The flag raisings did not mark a U.S. victory at Iwo Jima. But Rosenthal's photograph gave a morale boost to war-weary Americans, when news from the Pacific was often grim.

Americans were making sacrifices at home. To supply the war machine, the government rationed meat, cheese, milk, gasoline, rubber, and more.

The flag raisings showed Americans that their sacrifices for the war effort were small compared to those of the people defending the country.

The flag raisings and Rosenthal's image convinced Americans to remain committed to the struggle abroad. Adults bought billions of dollars of war bonds. Children collected scrap metal and donations in tin cans to support the war effort.

In 1945, Rosenthal won the Pulitzer Prize in photography for his famous photo. He died in 2006 at the age of 94. The photo is one of the most famous war photos ever taken. To this day it is among the most reproduced and inspirational images in U.S. history.

The flag raisings and the image sent a message of American hope, unity, and strength. Today, the handful of U.S. Marines atop Mount Suribachi represent all the men and women who struggled and served during World War II.

MORE ABOUT THE FLAG RAISING

- The six marines who raised the first flag were Lieutenant Harold Schrier, Sergeant Ernest Thomas, Sergeant Henry Hansen, Corporal Charles Lindberg, Hospital Corpsman John Bradley, and Private Philip Ward.

- At this time, the raisers of the second flag are officially identified as Corporal Harlon Block, Private Harold Keller, Private Franklin Sousley, Sergeant Mike Strank, Private Harold Schultz, and Private Ira Hayes. But Block, Schultz, and Keller were not originally identified in the photo. Sergeant Henry Hansen, Hospital Corpsman John Bradley, and Private René Gagnon were identified instead.

- In 1946, Belle Block, the mother of deceased Harlon Block, claimed that her son was in Rosenthal's photo. The Marine Corps investigated and concluded that the flag raiser identified as Henry Hansen was, in fact, Block.

- In 2014, history buffs Stephen Foley and Eric Krelle published evidence that John Bradley was not actually in Rosenthal's photo. After reviewing photos, letters, and unit rosters, the Marine Corps concluded that the man identified as Bradley was Harold Schultz.

- In 2019, a third Marine Corps investigation used modern scientific tools on photos and motion pictures of the second flag raising. It revealed that the marine identified as René Gagnon was actually Harold Keller.

- Nearly forgotten in the excitement created by Rosenthal's photo was the motion picture footage taken by Sergeant Bill Genaust. The grainy color film was used in newsreels and movie-length feature films. Genaust was declared killed in action on March 4. His body was never found. In 1995, a bronze plaque was placed atop Mount Suribachi in his honor.

- In addition to his service on Iwo Jima, Sergeant Louis Lowery had covered fighting on other Pacific islands including Guam and Saipan. He was awarded two Purple Hearts and earned the rank of captain after the war. Lowery's photo of the first flag raising remains an important record of the battle of Iwo Jima. Lowery died in 1987 at the age of 70.

- The two flags raised on Iwo Jima are housed at the National Museum of the Marine Corps in Triangle, Virginia.

GLOSSARY

abandon (uh-BAN-duhn)—to leave somewhere or someone and not return

allies (AL-ize)—people or countries that are on the same side during a war

battalion (buh-TAL-yuhn)—a large unit of soldiers

casualty (KAZH-uhl-tee)—someone who is injured, captured, killed, or missing in an accident, a disaster, or a war

correspondent (kor-uh-SPON-duhnt)—someone who reports for television, radio, or newspapers about a special subject or place

extinct (ik-STINGKT)—an extinct volcano does not erupt anymore

impenetrable (im-PEHN-uh-truh-bul)—impossible to pass through or enter

pillbox (PIL-box)—a small, partly underground concrete fort

ration (RASH-uhn)—to give out in limited amounts

recall (REE-kawl)—to officially be told to return to a place

resistance (ri-ZISS-tuhnss)—fighting back

souvenir (soo-vuh-NEER)—an object that you keep to remind you of a place, a person, or something that happened

summit (SUHM-it)—the highest point, the top

READ MORE

Daddis, Susan, and Michelle Jovin. *World War II in the Pacific.* Huntington Beach, CA: Teacher Created Materials, 2020.

Otfinoski, Steven. *The Battle of Iwo Jima: Turning the Tide of War in the Pacific.* Mankato, MN: Capstone Press, 2020.

Roberts, Russell. *World War II in the Pacific.* Lake Elmo, MN: Focus Readers, 2023.

INTERNET SITES

Britannica Kids: Iwo Jima
kids.britannica.com/students/article/Iwo-Jima/327346

Kidadl: Battle of Iwo Jima Facts
kidadl.com/facts/battle-of-iwo-jima-facts-history-summary-significance-and-dates

The National WWII Museum: Iwo Jima Fact Sheet
nationalww2museum.org/sites/default/files/2020-02/iwo-jima-fact-sheet.pdf

ABOUT THE AUTHOR

Nel Yomtov is an award-winning author of children's nonfiction books and graphic novels. He specializes in writing about history, current events, biography, architecture, and military history. He has written numerous graphic novels for Capstone, including the recent *School Strike for Climate, Journeying to New Worlds: A Max Axiom Super Scientist Adventure*, and *The 1899 Newsboys' Strike*. In 2020 he self-published *Baseball 100*, an illustrated book featuring the 100 greatest players in baseball history. Nel lives in the New York City area.

Author photo by Nancy Golden

ABOUT THE ILLUSTRATOR

Passionate comic book artist Eduardo Garcia works from his studio (Red Wolf Studio) in Mexico City with the help of his talented son, Sebastian Iñaki. He has brought his talent, pencils, and colors to varied projects for many titles and publishers such as Scooby-Doo (DC Comics), Spider-Man Family (Marvel), Flash Gordon (Aberdeen), and Speed Racer (IDW).

Illustrator photo by Eduardo Garcia